Animal Superpowers

SUPER STRENGTH

Joanne Mattern

RED CHAIR · PRESS ·

Animal Superpowers is produced and published by Red Chair Press:

Red Chair Press LLC   PO Box 333   South Egremont, MA 01258-0333

www.redchairpress.com

Publisher's Cataloging-In-Publication Data

Names: Mattern, Joanne, 1963-

Title: Super strength / Joanne Mattern.

Other Titles: Core content library.

Description: South Egremont, MA : Red Chair Press, [2019] | Series: Earth's amazing animals : animal superpowers | Includes glossary, Power Word science term etymology, fact and trivia sidebars. | Includes bibliographical references and index. | Summary: "Meet nature's super-strong superheroes! From insects that can pull 1,000 times their own weight to mighty mammals that can carry hundreds of pounds, Earth's animal kingdom is full of animals with amazing super strength."-- Provided by publisher.

Identifiers: LCCN 2018937241 | ISBN 9781634404259 (library hardcover) | ISBN 9781634404310 (ebook)

Subjects: LCSH: Muscle strength--Juvenile literature. | Animals--Juvenile literature. | Insects--Juvenile literature. | CYAC: Muscle strength. | Animals. | Insects.

Classification: LCC QP321 .M38 2019 (print) | LCC QP321 (ebook) | DDC 573.7/5--dc23

Illustrations by Tim Haggerty

Maps by Joe LeMonnier

Photo credits: iStock except Alamy pg. 14, 26

Printed in United States of America

102018 1P CGBS19

Table of Contents

Introduction

Many superheroes in books and movies have super strength. These heroes can stop a falling building and perform other feats of strength. Believe it or not, there are animals with super strength too. These animals use their arms, legs, claws, trunks, and even their teeth in an amazing show of power.

Why do animals need to be super strong? Super strength can help an animal catch its **prey**. It can also help them carry food and supplies. Super strength is also super helpful when animals are hunting or defending themselves from danger. No matter how you look at it, being super-strong is a great power to have! Let's take a look at some of the strongest animals on Earth. You'll be amazed at the things they can do!

The Strongest:
The Dung Beetle

It might sound crazy, but an insect is the strongest animal on Earth. The Super-Strong Award goes to the dung beetle. This little creature is a lot stronger than it looks. A dung beetle can lift and drag an object more than 1,100 times its own weight. That would be like a person pulling six full buses down the road!

Dung beetles are strong because they work out. Males have horns on top of their heads. They use these horns as weapons when they fight each other. Fighting is like a workout for these beetles, it helps them get stronger.

Now You Know!

Dung beetles live in forests and grasslands all over the world.

Female dung beetles do not have a horn on their head. But their bodies are very strong.

"Dung" is another word for poop. These beetles get their name because poop is their favorite food. That sounds gross, but there are little bits of undigested food in animal dung. These bits of food provide nutrition for the beetle.

So what do dung beetles do with the poop? They gather up bits of it. Then they roll the poop into a big ball and carry it home. Some kinds of dung beetles also live inside the poop ball. Others lay their eggs inside it.

Despite their yucky diet, many animals like to eat dung beetles. These **predators** include birds and foxes.

Now You Know!

Dung beetles can live for about three years.

Grab and Go: The Eagle

An eagle's talons

One minute you are a big fish or a wild cat minding your own business. The next minute, a large bird swoops down and grabs you. Even though you weigh a lot, the bird has no trouble flying while it carries you in its powerful claws. You have just met an eagle with its super-strong feet.

Eagles have big, powerful feet. Each foot ends in a sharp claw called a **talon**. An eagle's talons can carry up to four times its weight. A bald eagle can lift up a small deer!

Now You Know!

The harpy eagle is the strongest eagle in the world. The harpy lives in Central and South America.

Harpy eagle

The powerful bald eagle is found only in North America.

White-tailed eagle

Eagles have super-strong wings, too. An eagle can fly as high as 10,000 to 15,000 feet (3-4.5 km). They can also **glide** for hours. Even a bad storm doesn't bother an eagle. The bird just soars along on the powerful winds.

When they aren't flying, most eagles live in big nests. An eagle's nest is called an aerie. A bald eagle's nest can be up to five feet (1.5 m) wide and four feet (1.2 m) deep.

Eagles eat many different things. Fish, foxes, deer, raccoons, and rabbits all taste good to a hungry eagle.

A leaf-cutter ant nest is filled with
tunnels and can hold thousands of ants.

Leaf-cutter ants use their
jaws to carry things.

Small but Mighty:
The Leaf-Cutter Ant

A leaf-cutter ant doesn't look that strong. This insect is only about an inch (2.5 cm) long. But it can carry objects that are 50 times heavier than its own weight. Not only that, but the leaf-cutter ant doesn't carry leaves with its legs. It carries them in its mouth.

Leaf-cutter ants use their strong jaws to bite off pieces of leaves. Then they carry the leaves in their jaws by holding the leaves over their heads. Leaf-cutter ants bring the leaves on a long trip back to their homes. The ants use the leaves as food for **fungi** that grow in their nests. Then the ants eat the fungi.

A leaf-cutter ant's jaws have a lot of muscles. This helps them carry heavy loads. Their jaws can also **vibrate** 1,000 times a second. These movements give the ants an incredibly strong grip.

Leaf-cutter ants live in rain forests all over Central and South America. There are some colonies in southwestern Mexico and the United States as well. These ants keep the forest healthy by removing leaves and letting more sunlight reach the ground.

Now You Know!

Anteaters, armadillos, lizards, snakes, and birds all like to eat leaf-cutter ants.

CLOSED

NO TRESPASSING

Keep Out

Under Quarantine

GO AWAY

These leaf cutter ants collect
mango leaves for a nest.

Long and Strong:
The African Elephant

African elephants are the largest land animal in the world. An elephant can be more than 11 feet (3.4 m) tall and weigh up to 13,000 pounds (6,000 kg). So it's no surprise that these huge animals are also some of the strongest creatures on Earth. What might be surprising is which body part has a lot of super-strength. That part is the elephant's trunk.

An African elephant can use its trunk in many ways. An elephant's trunk has about 100,000 muscles and **tendons**. Those muscles let the elephant lift more than 750 pounds (340 kg).

Now You Know!

A baby elephant weighs about 200 pounds (90 kg) and is three feet (1 m) tall when it is born.

Now You Know!

An adult elephant can eat 300 pounds (135 kg) of food a day.

Elephants use their trunks for many things. They use them to smell, breathe, and drink. Elephants also make loud trumpeting noises through their trunks. And the trunk is how elephants get their food. They use it to pull leaves off trees. An elephant's strong **tusks** help it dig plants out of the ground or rip bark off of trees. That's right, these giant animals are **herbivores**. They only eat plants.

Female elephants are called cows. They live in **herds** with their babies and other female elephants. Male elephants, or bulls, usually live by themselves.

Silverback Mountain
Gorilla

Amazing Arms:
The Gorilla

Gorillas are big animals. They stand more than five feet (1.5 m) tall and weigh up to 440 pounds (200 kg). However, it's the arms that really give a gorilla incredible strength.

A gorilla's arms are very long. A male gorilla's arms can stretch out more than eight and a half feet (2.6 m) from fingertip to fingertip. A gorilla can carry hundreds of pounds. They are so strong they can even rip down trees to get the fruit growing up high. Gorillas also use their long, strong arms to swing easily from branch to branch.

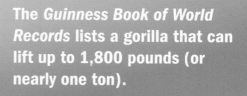

ALMOST ONE

TON

Now You Know!

The *Guinness Book of World Records* lists a gorilla that can lift up to 1,800 pounds (or nearly one ton).

Most gorillas eat fruit, tree bark, and bamboo. Some gorillas also eat ants and termites. They break open termite nests to eat the young insects inside. An adult gorilla eats up to 40 pounds (18 kg) of food a day.

Now You Know!
Only a few hundred mountain gorillas still live in the wild in Central Africa.

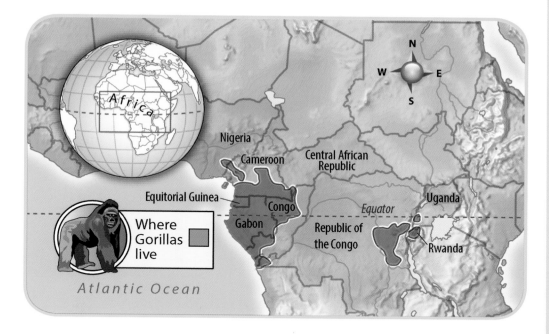

Nigeria

Cameroon

Central African Republic

Equitorial Guinea

Congo

Gabon

Equator

Uganda

Where Gorillas live

Republic of the Congo

Rwanda

Atlantic Ocean

Gorillas live in large groups. The oldest male is the leader. The rest of the **troop** includes several female gorillas and their children. Gorillas sleep in nests. These nests can be on the ground or high in the trees. Some gorillas build a new nest every night.

Big Bite:
The Grizzly Bear

One look at a grizzly bear and it's clear this is a very strong animal. This largest member of the bear family is almost ten feet (3 m) tall standing on its back legs. It weighs up to 600 pounds (270 kg). A grizzly's long, sharp claws are also strong. The animal uses them to grab prey such as fish or other animals.

One of the most powerful parts of a grizzly's body is its teeth. This big bear can bite down with incredible force. A grizzly's bite has a force of 1,200 pounds (545 kg) per square inch. That is strong enough to crush a bowling ball.

Grizzly bears live in the northwestern part of the United States and Canada.

Most of the grizzly bears in the United States are protected in national parks.

A grizzly bear eats many different foods. Its diet includes elk, fish, berries, and roots. It will even eat dead animals. In late summer, grizzlies start eating even more food. They need to store up fat for the winter.

Grizzlies spend most of the winter sleeping in caves or other sheltered places. Bears do not **hibernate** all winter and may wake up and go outside on a warm day. A female grizzly gives birth to one to four cubs during the winter. A cub only weighs about one pound (.5 kg) when it is born.

Power Word: Hibernate comes from *hiber*, the Latin word for winter.

Super-Strong Creatures

The animals in this book are among the strongest animals on our planet. They use their arms, horns, trunks, feet, teeth, and jaws to catch and carry food or perform other tasks. While the superheroes in movies and books use their powers to fight crime, these animals use their super strength just to stay alive.

It's fun to watch superheroes put on a display of super strength. But don't forget that animals in their natural habitat can be as strong as a superhero as well!

Glossary

fungi simple living things that reproduce by spores

glide to fly smoothly without flapping wings

herbivores animals that eat plants

herds large groups of animals that live and feed together

hibernate to be inactive during the winter

predator an animal that hunts other animals for food

prey animals that are hunted by other animals for food

talon a large, strong claw on a bird

tendons flexible tissue that attaches muscles to bones

troop a group of gorillas

tusks long, pointed teeth that stick out of an animal's mouth

vibrate to move back and forth very fast

Learn More in the Library

Albee, Sarah. *Amazing Animals: Elephants.* Gareth Stevens, 2009.

Bardoe, Cheryl. *Behold the Beautiful Dung Beetle.* Charlesbridge, 2014.

Nippert-Eng, Christena. *Gorillas Up Close.* Henry Holt & Co, 2016.

Index

About the Author

Joanne Mattern is the author of nearly 350 books for children and teens. She began writing when she was a little girl and just never stopped! Joanne loves nonfiction because she enjoys bringing science topics to life and showing young readers that nonfiction is full of compelling stories! Joanne lives in the Hudson Valley of New York State with her husband, four children, and several pets!